TRANSCENDING RACE IN AMERICA
BIOGRAPHIES OF BIRACIAL ACHIEVERS

Halle Berry

Beyoncé

David Blaine

Mariah Carey

Frederick Douglass

W.E.B. Du Bois

Salma Hayek

Derek Jeter

Alicia Keys

Soledad O'Brien

Rosa Parks

Prince

Booker T. Washington

SALMA HAYEK

Actress, Director, and Producer

Kerrily Sapet

Mason Crest Publishers

Produced by 21st Century Publishing and Communications, Inc.

MASON CREST PUBLISHERS INC.
370 Reed Road
Broomall, Pennsylvania 19008
(866) MCP-BOOK (toll free)
www.masoncrest.com

Printed in the United States of America.

First Printing

9 8 7 6 5 4 3 2 1

Library of Congress Cataloging-in-Publication Data

Sapet, Kerrily, 1972–
    Salma Hayek / Kerrily Sapet.
        p. cm. — (Transcending race in America)
    Includes bibliographical references and index.
    ISBN 978-1-4222-1616-3 (hardback : alk. paper) — ISBN 978-1-4222-1630-9 (pbk. : alk. paper)
    1. Hayek, Salma, 1968–   —Juvenile literature. 2. Actors—Mexico—Biography—Juvenile literature. I. Title. II. Series.
PN2318.H39S37 2009
791.4302'8092—dc22
[B]   2009027040

Table of Contents

"I HAVE BROTHERS, SISTERS, NIECES, NEPHEWS, UNCLES, AND COUSINS, OF EVERY RACE AND EVERY HUE, SCATTERED ACROSS THREE CONTINENTS, AND FOR AS LONG AS I LIVE, I WILL NEVER FORGET THAT IN NO OTHER COUNTRY ON EARTH IS MY STORY EVEN POSSIBLE."

"WE MAY HAVE DIFFERENT STORIES, BUT WE HOLD COMMON HOPES. . . . WE MAY NOT LOOK THE SAME AND WE MAY NOT HAVE COME FROM THE SAME PLACE, BUT WE ALL WANT TO MOVE IN THE SAME DIRECTION — TOWARDS A BETTER FUTURE . . ."

— BARACK OBAMA, 44TH PRESIDENT OF THE UNITED STATES OF AMERICA

Chapter 1

❀

A
STAR PRODUCER

AMERICA FELL IN LOVE WITH *UGLY BETTY*. Millions of TV viewers tuned in each week to watch the hit comedy on ABC. To Salma Hayek, co-executive producer of the show, *Ugly Betty* was a dream come true. The show changed attitudes about **Latin-American** actresses and proved brains triumph over beauty. Salma's hard work and determination had paid off.

Creating *Ugly Betty* fulfilled many of Salma's goals as a Mexican producer and actress. The series is an adaptation of the Colombian **telenovela** *Betty la fea*, (*Betty the Ugly One*), that has been rewritten into a New York City setting. The show tells the story of Betty Suarez, an unfashionable woman working for a fashion magazine. A Mexican woman, Betty struggles to succeed in a world prejudiced against her because of her race, culture, and looks. Salma related to the fictional character. In real life, she faced **racism**

Salma Hayek (right), co-executive producer of ABC's hit series *Ugly Betty*, appears in a scene with the show's star, America Ferrara. *Ugly Betty* was adapted from a Colombian show and has a Latino star and story line. The show's success was a triumph for Salma, capping years of hard work and determination.

as a Latin-American woman. Like Betty, she tackled obstacles and succeeded where others had not. Salma explained,

> **"**What I love about Betty is that she is a fighter, she has a sense of humor about herself, and she's more confident than anyone else around her. And in a country like ours, the U.S., which is so image-oriented, I wanted to see a show like that on television. I wanted to have a character that was just normal looking, or maybe even pretty, but to the standards only of this

country, not of the fashion industry that thinks she's ugly just because she's not skinny and tall. The name is actually sarcastic. **"**

America Loves America

Thick glasses. Bushy eyebrows. Mousy brown wig. Actress America Ferrara puts on her costume to become Betty Suarez. Like Salma, America Ferrara is a Latin-American actress. Her parents are from Honduras, although she grew up in California. She also had difficulty finding roles because of racism.

"I'm sure, like me, everyone told her, 'You'll never make it,'" Salma said. America Ferrara kept trying. Before *Ugly Betty*, she appeared in commercials and in the movie *The Sisterhood of the Traveling Pants*.

America Ferrara believes *Ugly Betty* is important because it portrays Mexican-American families differently. "They're not hitting piñatas every weekend," she said. Her character is a good role model too. She said, "When Betty does fail, she gets up and does it again, trying harder."

FAME AND FORTUNE

Emmy Awards, Golden Globes, and Academy Awards, or Oscars, are among the most prestigious awards an actress can win. In 2002, Salma became the first Mexican actress nominated for an Academy Award for Best Actress for her role in *Frida*. Her show *Ugly Betty* later captured three Emmys and two Golden Globes. It also won four American Latino Media Arts (ALMA) Awards, recognizing Salma's important contributions to the **Hispanic** community.

In the past 20 years, Salma has starred in more than 30 movies. She has appeared in dramas, comedies, thrillers, and action movies. Salma likes to play tough characters. Her roles on the big screen and on TV have included a vampire, an artist, a jewel thief, and a bearded lady in a circus.

Unlike many actresses, Salma has the skill to act, direct, and produce successful movies and TV shows. She is able to encourage new Latin-American actresses and provide them with opportunities. She also can create the stories she wants to tell, showing pride in her cultural background. Salma notes:

Salma presents an award at the 2007 Golden Globe Awards. That was a landmark night for Latinos because *Ugly Betty* won two awards: Best Comedy and Best TV Comedy Actress for America Ferrara. As a producer and director, Salma has broken stereotypes; Latin-American actresses have more opportunities in films and TV.

> **"If Hollywood won't give me the parts I want, I'm at the place where I can supply them for myself. Because I do believe in myself—even if they don't."**

Salma's talent has earned her millions of dollars. She has appeared on popular TV talk shows and been featured in magazines, newspapers, and advertisements around the world. On the

Salma's beauty was sometimes as much of an obstacle as her ethnic background when she was starting out as an actress. Through hard work and determination she has proved that as a Mexican actresses, she can handle any role, and produce and direct as well.

Internet, fans follow her career and personal life. They rush to see her latest movies. Despite her fame and fortune, Salma focuses on acting and making a difference in the world.

BREAKING DOWN BARRIERS

Salma has overcome many obstacles in her career when her race, heritage, and beauty often worked against her. In Hollywood, she often didn't receive parts because of racial discrimination and **stereotypes** about Mexican people. She said,

> **"People in this town know Mexicans only as maids. And they don't hesitate to tell you that when you're making a movie. I remember going to audition for a sci-fi film and the studio being aghast at the idea of a Mexican in space. One casting director even told me I should take advantage of my Middle-Eastern sounding name and pretend I was Lebanese."**

Salma also had trouble getting serious roles because of her looks. Directors decided she was too beautiful to play difficult characters. These obstacles only fueled her desire to succeed. Her years of hard work and determination helped her become the most powerful Mexican actress in Hollywood. Salma has always followed her dreams, doing all she can to bring them to life:

> **"I do dream hard, but I'm very flexible. I think it's the only way to be a true visionary. I don't think I'm going to fail, but if I do, the next person in the line will go a little bit further because I took the chance."**

2

A CHILDHOOD OF DIVERSITY

SALMA'S CHILDHOOD IN MEXICO WAS LIKE a vacation. She traveled, soaked up sunshine, and played in the ocean. She enjoyed her family's wealth and blend of cultures. Although Salma became a TV star in Mexico by the time she was in her twenties, fame and easy acting wasn't enough. She planned to prove herself as a serious actress in Hollywood.

FOLLOWING HER HEART

Salma Valgarma Hayek-Jiménez was born on September 2, 1966, in Coatzacoalcos, Mexico. Her father, Sami, was an oil businessman from Lebanon. Salma's mother, Diana, was an opera singer of Spanish descent. The family lived in a beautiful home, and Salma and her younger brother Sami had many pets, including a tiger. Salma remembers,

Salma had a happy childhood in the seaside town of Coatzacoalcos, Mexico. Her parents were of Lebanese and Spanish descent, and she enjoyed growing up with a mixture of cultures. From a very early age Salma knew she wanted to become an actress.

"I thought I was a princess. I lived in a castle and my father was a king. I wore tiaras. I was born diva-ish. When other kids were getting excited about toys, I would get excited about clothes."

On rainy afternoons, Salma loved going to the movies. After watching *Charlie and the Chocolate Factory*, she decided to become an actress. "Why would anyone want to do anything else in life?" she asked.

Salma was smart and confident, but being diagnosed with **dyslexia**, a learning disability that made reading difficult, fueled her desire to succeed. After graduating from high school, she studied acting. Although she was afraid people would laugh, Salma pursued her dream. She recalled,

> "I always wanted to be an actress ever since I was a little girl, but later I tried to convince myself that's not what I wanted. That I wanted to settle down with a stable career. That's what everyone else was doing, and it's what my parents expected of me. So, I tried to put that part of me away. But I couldn't fool myself."

Trouble with Words

Dyslexia affects millions of people. The learning disability makes reading, writing, spelling, and often math difficult. For people with dyslexia, letters, sounds, and numbers often get jumbled. Different teaching methods can help them learn to read and succeed in math.

Many famous people, including scientists, writers, and entertainers have dyslexia. Award-winning actor Tom Cruise and actress Whoopi Goldberg are just two. Orlando Bloom and Kiera Knightley, stars of *Pirates of the Caribbean*, are among many others.

People with dyslexia are intelligent. They often are good at reading emotions and have great memories. Those skills, plus determination and talent, are what makes an actress like Salma great.

SOAP OPERA STAR

At first, Salma appeared in commercials and had a small role on a Spanish-language soap opera, or telenovela. Then in 1989, she landed the starring role on the popular Mexican soap opera *Teresa*. Salma's ability impressed people. She won two Novela Awards, or Mexican Emmy Awards.

By this time Salma had money and fame. But she didn't want to be a soap opera star. As she explained later,

> "I was also afraid I was a very bad actress, because I'd become famous very fast and was making money for

people. When you're making money, they're never going to tell you whether you're good or bad. They don't care. I knew that if I had any talent, this would kill it.**99**

Salma owed herself and her fans more. She said, "If they're going to love me, I want to give them something really good." She decided to move to Hollywood where she could find more acting opportunities.

After high school, Salma followed her dream and became a soap opera star. Although she won awards and was successful, she wanted to become a better actress. Salma hoped to find more opportunities in Hollywood, so she moved there even though she could barely speak English.

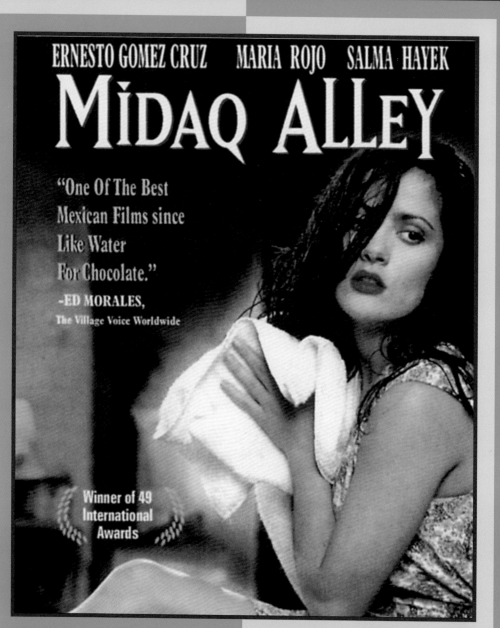

ERNESTO GOMEZ CRUZ   MARIA ROJO   SALMA HAYEK

MIDAQ ALLEY

"One Of The Best
Mexican Films since
Like Water
For Chocolate."
-ED MORALES,
The Village Voice Worldwide

Winner of 49
International
Awards

Salma had her first starring role in the Mexican film *Miracle Alley*. The movie was a huge success and won many international awards. Salma received award nominations, too. Her acting skill drew the attention of filmmaker Robert Rodriguez, who later cast her in several of his movies.

STARTING OVER

In 1991, Salma arrived in Hollywood but couldn't find a job. She spoke little English, and few people understood her Spanish **accent**. Everybody doubted Salma's decision. She recalled:

> "They would tell me to my face that I was crazy. . . . but I truly thank myself for following my dream. I wanted to be a very good actress. I wanted to do films."

Salma spent two years taking acting classes and studying English. She found few opportunities, though, and faced stereo types about Mexican women being maids and **immigrants**. So she returned to Mexico for a few months to star in the Mexican film *El Callejon de los Milagros* (*Miracle Alley*). Directed by Mexican filmmaker Jorge Fons, the movie was divided into four parts. Each section told the story of a different person who lived in a poor neighborhood in Mexico City.

The movie offered Salma her first starring role as Alma, a woman whose boyfriend moved to America hoping to find fortune. Her character struggled to escape poverty. Salma liked that the movie showed the difficult lives of poorer people in Mexico. She also enjoyed the opportunity to make a movie in her **native** country. It gave her more experience in the movie-making industry. Salma said,

> "It would have been easier to just stay in Hollywood, but there are a lot of exciting things happening in Mexican cinema. I feel proud of it and I want to support it."

After returning to the U.S., Salma appeared on a talk show and discussed the discrimination Hispanic actresses faced. Her attitude impressed filmmaker Robert Rodriguez. He offered her a leading role in his movie, *Desperado*. Salma's career in Hollywood was ready to take off.

Chapter

3

❀

TAKING OFF

SALMA HAD STARTED HER HOLLYWOOD career at zero. But her talent, beauty, and determination impressed director Robert Rodriguez, who offered her a leading role in the film *Desperado*. The wildly successful movie jump-started Salma's career. In the next five years, she would take Hollywood by storm, starring in dozens of movies.

JUMP-STARTING HER CAREER

Desperado told the story of a singer, played by Antonio Banderas, who was mistaken for a drug dealer. Salma played his girlfriend, a bookstore owner named Carolina. She enjoyed filming the **stunts** for the action movie. When the film premiered in the summer of 1995, it was a box office hit. So was Salma. She was on the road to fame, and she had big plans:

Salma and co-star Antonio Banderas appear in a dramatic scene from the 1995 movie *Desperado*. The film helped Salma's career take off, and her reputation as a talented actress blossomed. She was also proud to represent Mexican culture to American audiences.

"If I'm starting all over again, then I have the opportunity to represent not just my own talents but also my entire culture to a whole new audience."

Later that year, Salma's work in *Miracle Alley* brought her worldwide fame. The movie won 50 awards internationally, more than any other film made in Mexico. Salma was nominated for a Silver Ariel Award, a Mexican Academy Award, for Best Actress. Many people call *Miracle Alley* one of Mexico's greatest films.

BEAUTY AND BRAINS

Salma soon landed more roles. Her partnership with Robert continued. She played a dancer in his movie *Four Rooms.* Then she took a role in *Fair Game*, starring as the girlfriend of a policeman. In 1996, she played a female vampire in Robert's movie *From Dusk Till Dawn.* In the creepy thriller, she had to overcome her fear of snakes to dance with a python. Although the movie received mixed reviews, she was developing a reputation as an actress.

Salma appears with award-winning film director Robert Rodriguez, who helped jump-start her career by casting her in several of his movies. Robert was one of the first people in Hollywood to believe in Salma's talent. He says he always thinks of her when he is casting a new movie.

Making Movie Magic

Robert Rodriguez's career began when his family bought a video camera. As a young boy, his movies usually featured his nine siblings. Today, Robert works with Hollywood's biggest stars. A director, producer, and writer, he is a respected Latino film-maker. He has made more than 26 movies and won several awards. Many of his films are set in Mexico or Texas and are famous for their creativity and quick camera movements.

Robert was the first Hollywood filmmaker who believed in Salma. The two have a close bond. They have worked together on several movies, including *Desperado* and *Spy Kids-3D*. He commented, "I always consider Salma for my projects, even for male roles."

Audiences found Salma beautiful, but she had learned an important lesson about looks at a young age. When she worried about being short, her father had told her, "Intelligence is not measured from your feet to your head, it is measured from your head to the infinite."

Salma learned that intelligence and talent were more valuable than beauty or height. She wanted to be more than just an attractive actress and was frustrated when studio executives resisted giving her roles that portrayed smart women.

Salma also continued to face stereotypes because she was a biracial Mexican actress. Her accent and the color of her skin limited the parts directors would give her. The stereotypes and racism made her angry. She recalled,

> **"Hollywood made a very big effort not to let me in . . . they had a very specific image for Mexicans that I didn't quite fit. Mexicans are gang members, on welfare with kids since they were 15, and they wear make-up and they're tacky and cheesy. They think we're uneducated and have no sense of style."**

A RISING STAR

Salma wasn't going to give up. She soon landed a small part in the movie *Fled*. Next, she co-starred with Russell Crowe in *Breaking Up*, the story of a couple that fought constantly. It was the first role

Salma shares a scene with co-star Russell Crowe in *Breaking Up*. Her performance in the film showed the world that she could play any type of character. Salma continued to prove herself by appearing in many smaller, independent movies instead of big Hollywood productions.

Salma received that wasn't written specifically for a Hispanic woman. She said, "People told me I was wrong for the part so, of course, I said, 'Perfect.'" Her performance proved her ability to play different types of characters.

As more opportunities came Salma's way, she could choose her roles carefully. Often she passed up parts in big movies to star in smaller films. She said, "I'd rather have a small part in a good movie than a starring role in a bad one." Salma remained loyal to Robert Rodriguez. She landed a role in his movie *The Mask of Zorro*. However, when he abandoned the project, she too backed away.

Salma kept busy with new projects. In *Fools Rush In*, she played a Mexican woman in an interracial relationship and starred opposite Matthew Perry, a popular TV star. Salma helped change the **script** so her character better represented her culture. Not only was the movie a success, but Salma also learned more about how a movie was put together. She was nominated for an ALMA Award for her role, recognizing her ability as a Latin-American actress. The support of her community was important to her:

> **"They embraced me and were with me when I was doing my first soap opera. They didn't know me, but they believed in me. Since I began at the bottom of Hollywood, that has given me a lot of strength."**

Next, Salma played Esmeralda, an enchanting gypsy, in *The Hunchback*. The movie was based on the book *The Hunchback of Notre Dame*. On the set, she met actor Edward Atterton, and the two soon began dating.

BREAKING DOWN STEREOTYPES

Salma's beauty and glamour continued to bring her attention. In 1997, she became a **spokesperson** for Revlon, one of the world's largest cosmetics companies. Although Salma enjoyed fashion, looking beautiful was important to her for other reasons. She wanted to prove that Mexican women had style. She wore a beautiful beaded dress and diamond tiara to the Academy Awards. She even dressed up for a casual show on MTV. Salma explained,

> **"I've made a conscious choice to put a lot of effort into it. Not only because it's creative for me, but also to break a little bit of the stereotype of Mexicans being tacky people, lazy people, with no taste and no style. It's not who we really are. It's important for me to show that we don't wear *huaraches* [Mexican leather sandals] and sombreros all day long."**

Salma looks stunning as she arrives at the 1997 MTV Movie Awards. She always looked glamorous and wanted to show that Mexican women could be very stylish. She even appeared in Revlon cosmetic advertisements, but her main focus continued to be on acting.

Salma appeared in Revlon advertisements but remained focused on acting. More movies soon followed. In 1998, she took a role in the teen horror movie *The Faculty*. She also starred in *54*, a movie about a famous nightclub in the 1970s, playing a girl who dreams of becoming a singer. Although the movie was a flop, she enjoyed filming it and wearing outrageous costumes from the 1970s. She also starred in the romantic comedy *The Velocity of Gary*, playing a tough waitress.

BIGGER ROLES, BIGGER MOVIES

Salma began to land parts in movies with bigger stars. In 1999, she took a role in the movie *Dogma*. Famous actors Matt Damon and Ben Affleck also starred in the movie, playing angels who were expelled from heaven. The movie followed their struggles to get back into heaven. Salma played a muse, or beautiful woman who inspired music, art, and writing. However, her character, named Serendipity, had trouble. Her creative writing ability failed her as long as she remained on Earth.

Salma appeared in the movie *Dogma* with big-name actors Matt Damon and Ben Affleck. That year she was also in a film with Will Smith and impressed the director with her acting talent. Salma was being noticed, and she began to be offered bigger parts in bigger movies.

The movie *Dogma* was **controversial**. Many people believed the film made fun of religion, and some sent the filmmaker threatening letters. Protesters lined up outside theaters, trying to discourage people from watching the movie. Their attitudes didn't bother Salma. She was proud of her work in the movie.

Friends and Filmmakers

Growing up together in Boston, Matt Damon and Ben Affleck planned to become actors. After writing the script for a movie called *Good Will Hunting*, their dreams came true. The movie, about a janitor who is a math genius, was a tremendous success. The two actors won Academy Awards for Best Screenplay. Matt Damon said,

"*Good Will Hunting* is so close to my heart because my best friend and I invented him."

Matt Damon and Ben Affleck have starred together in many films. They also have made popular movies separately. With their company Pearl Street Productions, they hope to one day produce another box office hit together.

That same year, Salma also appeared in *Wild Wild West*. The movie, modeled after a 1960s TV show, combined action, science fiction, and comedy. The star-studded cast included Kevin Kline and Will Smith. Salma played the beautiful Rita Escobar. The three teamed up to capture Dr. Arliss Loveless, an evil genius attempting to attack the U.S. president with a giant mechanical spider. On the movie set, Salma impressed the film's director so much that he increased her number of scenes from two to 18.

Despite costly special effects and massive marketing, *Wild Wild West* flopped at the box office. It won five Golden Raspberry Awards, or Razzies, for being the worst movie of the year. However, Salma's performance earned her a Blockbuster Award.

MAKING HER MARK

Salma was one of the few Latin-American actresses in Hollywood finding success on the big screen. Despite her achievements, many directors still considered her race and accent before casting her. Some people said attitudes in Hollywood were changing towards minorities, but Salma disagreed,

Salma proudly displays her 2000 Blockbuster Award. She was one of the few Latin-American actresses who was successful in Hollywood, but she wanted more parts to be available for all Latin actresses. She founded her own production company, and her career took a whole new turn.

> **"I don't believe in the so-called Latino explosion when it comes to movies. . . . I grew up in Mexico, not the U.S., and the fact is that there just aren't any parts for Latin actresses. I have to persuade people that my accent won't be a problem, but an asset. Everyone's afraid of doing something a bit risky."**

Salma decided to form Ventanarosa, her own production company. Ventanarosa is Spanish for "rose-colored window." With her movies, Salma could provide opportunities for Latin-American actresses and break stereotypes about Mexican people. One critic called her "Central Station for Mexican filmmakers." Ventanarosa's first movie was *No One Writes to the Colonel.* Filmed in Mexico, it told the story of a poor, retired Mexican colonel. Salma played Julia, a woman in a relationship with the colonel's son. Many critics called it the best film of the year. The movie was nominated for a foreign-language Oscar and won several other awards.

As a producer and actress, Salma worked long days and traveled around the world. She appeared in newspapers and on the covers of magazines, such as *George*, a popular political magazine. The year 2000 was demanding. She played a young actress in *Time Code* and a detective in *Chain of Fools.* In *La Gran Vida*, she was a waitress who met a millionaire. Next came a small role in *Traffic*, a

The Melting Pot

America is sometimes called a melting pot. It means that people from different countries, races, religions, and cultures have come together to form one country. Today, the U.S. is more diverse than ever. Approximately one out of every six people is Hispanic. They represent the fastest-growing population in the country.

For hundreds of years, people have moved from all over the world to America in search of better lives. These immigrants often struggle to learn English and find jobs. Sometimes they face discrimination. Attitudes are changing, though. Many famous people—athletes, musicians, movie stars, and America's president, Barack Obama—are of different races and have roots in other countries. They prove that ability and determination are more important than skin color or heritage.

Salma appears with co-star Steve Zahn in a scene from the 2000 movie *Chain of Fools*. She worked nonstop that year, also appearing in *Timecode*, *La Gran Vida*, and *Traffic*. As an actress and producer she traveled widely and appeared in newspapers and magazines all over the world.

crime drama about the illegal drug trade. The film was nominated for an Oscar for Best Picture. The following year she appeared in the movie *Hotel*.

Although Salma was busy, she took time to help less fortunate people. She used her fame and wealth to help causes that were important to her. She took part in the Revlon Run/Walk for Women, an event that raised money to research cancer, a deadly disease afflicting millions. She also urged people to donate money to aid people affected by a devastating flood in Mexico.

HER NATIVE COUNTRY

As a Mexican actress and producer, Salma wanted to illustrate the beauty and history of her heritage. Her 2001 project, *In the Time of the Butterflies*, gave her the chance to share the true story of four legendary sisters from Latin America. She related the characters to her own story:

Salma (right) struggles with soldiers in a scene from *In The Time of Butterflies*, which she also produced. She was excited to film most of the movie in Mexico. Salma was proud of her efforts on the film and critics agreed; she won an ALMA Award for Outstanding Actress.